A FOREST
OF NAMES

A FOREST
OF NAMES

108 Meditations

IAN BOYDEN

WESLEYAN UNIVERSITY PRESS
MIDDLETOWN, CONNECTICUT

Wesleyan Poetry

Wesleyan University Press
Middletown CT 06459
www.wesleyan.edu/wespress

Manufactured in Canada
Typeset in Bembo, Futura, Songti, and Helvetica
Printed on #70 Rolland Enviro Satin. This paper is acid free,
contains 100% post-consumer fiber, and is manufactured using
renewable energy—Biogas and processed chlorine free. It is FSC®
and Ancient Forest Friendly™ certified.

Library of Congress Cataloging-in-Publication Data
Names: Boyden, Ian H., author.
Title: A forest of names : 108 meditations / Ian Boyden.
Description: Middletown : Wesleyan University Press, 2020. |
    Series: Wesleyan poetry | Includes index. | Summary: "Poems
    meditating on the names of children lost in the 2008 Sichuan
    Earthquake" — Provided by publisher.
Identifiers: LCCN 2020003827 (print) | LCCN 2020003828 (ebook) |
    ISBN 9780819579942 (hardcover) | ISBN 9780819579959 (trade
    paperback) | ISBN 9780819579966 (ebook)
Subjects: LCSH: Wenchuan Earthquake, China, 2008—Poetry. |
    LCGFT: Poetry.
Classification: LCC PS3602.O9343 F67 2020 (print) | LCC PS3602.O9343
    (ebook) | DDC 811/.6—dc23
LC record available at https://lccn.loc.gov/2020003827
LC ebook record available at https://lccn.loc.gov/2020003828

5 4 3 2 1

Frontispiece and title page images:
All of the names of schoolchildren gathered from "Names of the
Student Earthquake Victims Found by the Citizens' Investigation"
(2008–2011). Courtesy of Ai Weiwei Studios.

for Gavia Lachen

Contents

Beichuan County, Sichuan, May 2008. Photograph by Ai Weiwei.
Image courtesy of Ai Weiwei Studios.

Prologue

*A*T 2:28 ON MAY 12, 2008, an 8.0 earthquake
leveled western Sichuan province in China,
displacing millions of people and killing tens of
thousands of others. It was one of the deadliest
earthquakes in human history. It became clear
that a disproportionate number of schoolchildren
were killed when their government-built schools
collapsed on them. To conceal the corruption
behind the faulty construction, the government
prevented parents and citizens from finding out
who died, how many, and why—often using
brutal tactics. Despite this, artist and human
rights activist Ai Weiwei created a team called
Citizens' Investigation, which gathered and
published the names of the children. In total, this
list includes 5,196 names, their age, gender, date
of birth, and which school they attended.

WHAT am I, after all, but a child, pleased with the
    sound of my own name? repeating it over and over,
I cannot tell why it affects me so much, when I hear
    it from women's voices, and from men's voices,
    or from my own voice,
I stand apart to hear—it never tires me.

To you, your name also,
Did you think there was nothing but two or three
    pronunciations in the sound of your name?

—Walt Whitman, "Leaves of Grass," 1860–61

Those children have parents, dreams, and they
could smile, they had a name that belonged to
them. That name will belong to them three years
from now, five years, eighteen or nineteen years
later; it is everything about them which may be
remembered, it is everything that might be evoked.

—Ai Weiwei, March 20, 2009

Zhèngxī

正曦
First Glimmer of Dawn

Even the moon was shaken.
How the dust settled so quickly.

The people looked to where
the sun should rise, waited
as if it were an offering.

They held the place
where they thought their heart should be
though there was no proper place.

Stones, parts of buildings,
papers scattered like leaves.

It must be winter,
but the trees say it is late spring.

The horizon of her name,
dark blue but fading.

Péi

培
Banked with Earth

Where continuity consists of brokenness,
we plant the seeds of forget-me-nots.

MAY 21

Yuèxīn

月新
Made New by the Moon

She came with her chisels and carved,
month after month, until the tree

was a thousand feet of moonlight.

Xiùpín

秀頻
Perennial Inflorescence

Walk the wild meadows of late May.
With the slightest wind,
her name sweeps the sky.

峿晨
Island Daybreak

Hands ring the isolate of earth
where her name lies buried in the morning sun.
She was four.

Jìtáo

濟陶
Crossing the River of Delight

Wind crosses the ripening field
like a hand across raw clay.

The first gift
a name the texture of infinity.

JUNE 1

Shuǎng

爽
Clear and Crisp

The dictionary fell open,
a single word
offering autumn light.

Then, as now,
her name cradles the broken
and unbroken lines of divination.

JUNE 3

Zhuō

卓
Outstanding Divination

Because the reading is also a becoming,
in his name there stands
a person who reads these texts—

A cloud's color within the arc of a bird's flight.

The chattered cracks in bone at fire's edge.

JUNE 4

Xiǎoyù

曉鈺

Daybreak Treasure

One jade dawn,
instead of searching the horizon,
she walked the limitless shore
of her own waking.

JUNE 9

Fēifēi

飛飛
Profusion of Wings

Her name an invisible bird—
waiting to take flight

from each mouth that called for her.

JUNE 12

Chéng

誠
Sincerity

If I am to be completed by words,
let them be the words of earth
and not of abdication.

JUNE 14

Míngkūn

明坤
Elucidate Earth

Plant a field of lightning.
Who will harvest the fruit?

瀚拱
Encircling Vast Ocean

Imagine your heart as a brush.
What would you write with it?

Its tidal ink caressing the shore.

JUNE 20

Shijūn

世均
Age of Equality

It didn't have to be a flower.
He could have presented a single leaf.

Shuāngshuāng

雙雙

Double Pair

She dreamt of a tree and woke
to two birds nesting in her left hand
and two in her right.

JULY 2

Xióngyì

熊毅
Resolute Bear

One star for each year he lived,
circling our hearts like a long-handled spoon.

JULY 10

Chénlín

陳林
Narrator of Forests

The forest seemed limitless, rising, leafing,
a fluid temple upon the undulating earth.

JULY 17

Bīn

彬
Refined

As she wrote, a line of trees
branched the blue void.

On the earth below,
we read the shadow of her mind.

JULY 19

Xiào

笑
Smile

The hills were an anchor of pleasure.
Young bamboo. Tender.
Bending this way and that in riotous wind.

Yínzhì

寅志

The Mark of the Third Earthly Branch

He was all tigers, and yet . . .
something in the shadows made him tremble.

JULY 24

Yànmíng

晏銘
Cloudless Inscription

Carved into stone, into the sky's edge.
Shadows rolled, but never across his name.

Tāo

濤
Wave of Longevity

It'll cross an entire ocean
long, white hair when it breaks

on the far shore.

Tiántián

甜甜
Sweet Sweet

A name rolling with melons,
hives of honey,
fields of sugar cane . . .
but none sweeter than the child's laugh.

Tiānwēi

天威
Celestial Awe

He carried no iron into battle.
When he lifted his hand,
he brandished the sky.

AUGUST 3

Zilíng

子凌
Child of Thick Ice

What glaciers within your heart?
Slow. Unremitting. Melting, calving.
At the edge: sapphire blue.

Bèi

蓓
Flower Bud

Held so quietly,
they failed to call her name.

Still, she sat
and waited for the thunder.

AUGUST 6

Fúléi

拂雷
Brush Away Thunder

The trees splintered.
But in his field, all was quiet.
No one had ever seen such a broom.

AUGUST 7

Méiyī

梅一
Plum Flower Singularity

Her name a strangelet,
converting each who called to her
into a swirl of blossoms.

AUGUST 9

Qiūmàn

秋曼
Autumn Vast and Beautiful

The ducks swam through the reflections
of trees and marsh grass,
with no thought of flying south.

AUGUST 12

Lín

林
Forest

The forest bisected as if by a mirror.
And yet the bird that flies from tree to tree
does not arc through its own reflection.

AUGUST 13

Yúntāo

雲濤
Cloud Wave

The limestone bones coil
an endless wave of question marks.

The clouds fade
but the questions do not.

AUGUST 20

Quányí

銓怡
Measured Harmony

Her heart upon a dais.
It is said our lives will be measured
against the weight of a feather.

AUGUST 26

Wéi

唯
Only

Even now
if you call her name
you'll become a singing bird.

Sēnlín

森林
Infinity of Trees

Once planted, the name proliferated.
Today, desert sand fills
around the ancient trunks.

Any footprints quickly disappear.

SEPTEMBER 3

Hóngchén

鸿臣

Minister of the Swan

Eye of the storm
that brings the flood
and leaves behind
a single white feather.

Yǐng

穎
Tassel

Have you listened
to the love song of the wind?

It trembles every blade,
the mind of the meadow at play.

SEPTEMBER 9

Mínghào

銘皓
Inscription of Luminosity

The autumn spider weaves its inscriptions
with dew, with shifting light.

It may not yet have caught an insect,
but it has caught my heart.

SEPTEMBER 11

Bóyǔ

博宇
Erudite Universe

The far edge of the ringing bell
is also the soft edge of the hand
that struck it.

Chónglín

崇林
Forest of Veneration

She knelt before the mountain,
to all sides, the forest of her ancestors—
a long lineage that ended with her name.

Xiùméi

秀梅
Flourishing Plum

We scarcely noticed
the tree writing its poem
until the last lines
filled with golden light.

Then we eyed the dark birds
gathering to the fruit.

Sīyǔ

思語
Language of Thought

She became a reflection of words,
an expression of language,
even after the harrowing
of the heart's field.

Shùnháng

順航
Navigator of Coherence

Whomever could cut
enough corners to collapse
a school is beyond the reach of this name.

OCTOBER 1

Jǐngyú

景瑜
Lustrous Field

Hold it close. Recall
looking into your child's eyes the first time.

OCTOBER 6

Lóngqiáng

龍強

Dragon-vigor

Tell us what was written with your shadow.

Long after the cicada's song
enters autumn's soil, the brittle husks
that once held their singing bodies
still hold dearly to the branches
where they once sang.

Sēnyàn

森燕

Swallow within the Infinity of Trees

And in that northern kingdom
a single prince faced the tyranny
that never ends.

藝豪
Heroic Art

He kneads the earth
and earth measures his absence.

Studies of impossible form
rise above brittle structures
of our failing.

Dié

蝶
Butterfly

Autumn wings, the wind.
Somewhere there's a tree,
whose every leaf dreams of flight.

OCTOBER 16

Yŏulì

友櫟

Friend of the Oak

Outstretched hands
overflowing with acorns.

OCTOBER 22

Qiānyú

芊榆

Luxuriant Elm

A thousand leaves quivering yes, yes.
And the boat, dreaming of water,
grows within the tree.

OCTOBER 23

Zéyǒng

澤泳
Swim the Lustrous Pool

In the still morning,
the remote pond is a plate of silver
made molten by ducks.

OCTOBER 29

Kě

可
Possible

Cup and plate get set each evening.

NOVEMBER 3

Zōnglì

宗麗

Ancestor of Beauty

This altar within the antlers of a living deer—
lightning cloaked in velvet.

NOVEMBER 4

Xīlíng

溪玲
Mountain Stream Ringing Jade

She plucked the strings of cold water,
each green sound calling: now, now, now.

NOVEMBER 5

Yèkāi

葉開
Opening Leaf

As it opened, they saw written across
its heart this single word:

world.

NOVEMBER 9

Yīngjié

英傑
Distinguished Flower

He called to the butterflies.
This field, he said, is filled with heroes.

Zǐyǔ

姿羽
Disposition of a Wing

Within the storm,
the gulls break
the ink–black sky.

They reassemble for shattering.

Chéngfēi

成飛
To Become Flight

The sweet light of such becoming—
persimmons litter the ground
of a forgotten garden.

Guān

観
Observe

A grey-blue bodhisattva
with a thousand wings,
each with a thousand feathers,
stands utterly still.

With eyes of a child
it attends to the flowing world.

NOVEMBER 27

Bō

波
Ripple

Perhaps we are the skin of something
whose body we don't know how to see.

Yuánpéng

園鵬
Orchard Peng

The great bird danced
on the flowering branches
as if it would never return
to taste the fruit.

DECEMBER 1

Zhènghán

正函

Just Correspondence

The tongue like a bow.

Even after a thousand years,
words chosen carefully
still hit their mark.

DECEMBER 2

Xuětíng

雪庭
Snow Courtyard

The hand of snow upon the gavel.
A white sentence under a dark sky
beyond innocence and guilt.

Zhìwén

志雯
Marked by the Writing of Clouds

She was born a blank page
where shadows played.

A poem brushed by the sky.

DECEMBER 9

Dōngling

冬玲
Winter Ringing

The earth rows its boat around the sun,
striking the drum of winter,
its wake deafening white.

Bīnháng

彬航

Refined Boat

The helmsman wanders the forest,
following oar marks
on moss-covered ground.

DECEMBER 15

Fēi

菲

Fragrant Radish

It grew with such delight,
red heart of soil,
its roots tangled
in a bird's broken wings.

Dàiyáng

代揚
Dynastic Scatter

The dandelion's silver
floats on our breath,
each flower a measure
of the sun-tossing hand.

DECEMBER 27

Lǐliàng

禮亮

Luminosity of Offering

A dragonfly wing
filled with moonlight.

Zhījǐn

芝瑾

Mushroom of Virtuosity

One can walk for years
and never find one,
glowing dark purple
beyond the spectrum of our mind.

長花
Long Flower

The honeysuckle could endure
the heavy bloom of winter,
but not the walls of the school's collapse.

Shīmèng

詩夢
Poem Dream

"Poem Dream," they called.
And everything answered,
"Yes, I'm here,"

even the dust
settling in raw sunlight.

JANUARY 7

Jīnpíng

金萍
Golden Duckweed

Heavier than air,
lighter than water.
Fish rest in her shadows.
A frog sunbathes on her back!

Shèngxīn

盛鑫

Ladleful of Infinite Gold

What the spoon held
was our mind of starlight,
spinning but never empty
and never full.

JANUARY 21
Yǔhàn

雨菡
Lotus Bud in Rain

That morning, the petals' opening
sounded like an envelope
torn by a shaking hand.

Xuěyàn

雪燕
Snow Swallow

Long after the others had flown
one wing-black spiral
through ice-white air.

Xuělián

雪蓮
Snow Lotus

To the cicadas, mosquitoes,
and rattling wings of the humid air—

the mud offers
pure white hands.

Yì

易
Change

He tried. He was a child.
No one ever said,
just as you are.
Just, as you are.

Xuān

萱
Daylily

She slowly forgot her worries,
wandering the limitless halls of sunlight.

FEBRUARY 1

Míngjìng

明靜
Motionless Clarity

There, where moonlight spills
across a handful of ash.

FEBRUARY 2

Lù

霽

Clearing Sky

He stood on his head,
and to his astonishment
watched the clouds ripening
like fields of grain.

Guānyǔ

關宇

Barrier / Cosmos

The ageless subject of Chan meditation:
How to pass through one's own name?

Xiǎosēn

小森
Small Forest

Once finished with the trunk,
the brush dances side to side.

An infinity of black
from the heart
of a burning pine.

FEBRUARY 10

Miáomiáo

苗苗
Sprout Sprout

And from the same quarry
that lined the mausoleum of a tyrant,
the blocks of marble were carved
into a field of white grass.

FEBRUARY 12

Zhǐjūn

沚君
Sandbar Lord

The edges of his heart,
written by the footprints of plovers,
anchored by love,
washed by rain.

Rénkǎi

仁鍇

Humane Iron

Pulled from the wreckage,

the rebar appeared to cradle
what it held.

Shūchéng

書晟

Book of Solar Luminosity

Once bound, the book
could never be held,
could never be read—

what it offered
was the light
of its own transformation.

Hànmò

瀚墨
Vast Ink

At sunrise,
the white feather fell
from an empty sky.

Now blackened
with a century of burning,
it erases the stars.

Línyíng

林萤
Forest of Fireflies

For a lifetime we pulsed
messages of light into the void, and waited,

until we understood our message
was also our answer.

Sīyǔ

思宇
Universe of Thought

Always hovering,
a field suspended
above the heart.

But what held
the thought aloft
was no match
for the shelter
of its finality.

Yŭxuě

羽雪
Feather Snow

This name is so quiet.
It waits for the wind.

The child's down pillow still
waits for its dreamer.

Yǔhán

宇涵
Saturated Universe

A lifetime of letters spilled
into the Min River.

Helpless to gather them
she drank the ink-blackened water.

MARCH 15

Shūyuān

淑淵
Pure Abyss

Slowly shifting shadows of light—
the only record of distant waves.

MARCH 17

Chényǔ

晨雨
Daybreak Rain

We blackened the first brush tip
to draw this very image.

We haven't set the brush down since.

She was five.

MARCH 26

Xiǎolì

小麗
Small Beauty

In honor of small beauty,
recognize where it exists.

Qiǎolì

巧麗
Coincidental Beauty

Coincident with 5,195 other beauties.

MARCH 31

Hǎi

海
Ocean

His name was both a boat
and the water upon which it drifted.

A white boat dissolved
into a white horizon.

APRIL 2

Chén

晨
Daybreak

The sun with its plow;
the mind with its act.

APRIL 8

Qīngjīng

清菁
Pure Essence

When her name left your lips,
a leek flower opened over dark water.

Even her name had a moon.

Wànróng

萬容
Myriad Container

The urn shattered,
ten thousand questions scattered
in the stone dust.
But each in its own way asked,

Are we still one?

宴仙
Immortal Feast

Mayhem:
iridescent fungi,
numinous deer,
too many peaches,
giant carp upsetting the table . . .

Jiànchuān

建川
Builder of Rivers

Let this page describe what it saw
in the Blue River,
the River of the Mountain People.

A black pattern emerged out of emptiness,
like a name out of the silence
from which we were born.

Qīyǔ

漆宇
Lacquer Cosmos

What is this mind
like a bucket of black lacquer?

Dark liquid of pure light
where one sees without seeing.

We paint the coffin
with the blood of trees—

a thousand days of sunlight.

APRIL 20

Miǎo

森
Infinity

Your name a molecule,
wind bound to stone.

Every drop of this river
once fell from the sky.

Xuělíng

雪苓

Snow Fungus

The soil-woven
sing within spring mountains:

dark flowers at the edge of ice.

Dēnglì

登麗

The Ascent of Beauty

She climbed, each step a quiet drum.
Antlers bleaching among spring wildflowers.

Wénlín

文林
Literary Forest

Where the full moon once cast
shadows of woven branches,

the new moon looks upon barren ground.

MAY 10

Yìlín

一霖

At One with Copious Rain

One with parted cloud,
with leaf-drummed birdsong
of swirling vapor and swollen river,

one with fallen stone.
Now one with memory itself
in the delicate halls of language.

MAY 12

Hàolán

浩瀾
Vast Swelling Waves

He died on his eighth birthday.

They drew the number eight—
the figure of infinity.

They drew the number
as a map,
and waited for their son
at the crossroads.

They drew it
as if it were his name,
a locked door,
a letter,
orchid-like within the water.

His absence an abyss.
Today, may his name overflow.

Beichuan County, Sichuan, May 2008. Photograph by Ai Weiwei.
Image courtesy of Ai Weiwei Studios.

Epilogue

IN JANUARY 2016, I CURATED the exhibition *Ai Weiwei: Fault Line*, which explored Ai Weiwei's response to the 2008 Wenchuan earthquake. One of the works included in this exhibition was the list of the 5,196 names of schoolchildren killed in it. Installing this piece required that I paste, by hand, 21 scrolls of delicate paper across 42 feet of the museum's walls. The process took several days, and as I did so, I marveled at the poetry of the names: First Glimmer of Dawn, Cloudless Inscription, Disposition of a Wing, Humane Iron. Reading the names in the quiet of the museum felt like an evocation.

In addition to Ai Weiwei collecting the names, he also gathered hundreds of tons of twisted iron rebar from the collapsed schools. He carved exact facsimiles of several of those twisted pieces of rebar out of marble and made coffins for them. Iron—ductile, dense, industrial, and opaque—is transformed into a stone—fragile, cherished, and luminescent. Delicate bones of the earth. The image on the cover of this book is one of these pieces, and it presents a challenge to others to see what they can make of tragedy, of how they can insist on a system that values responsibility.

What might I learn from these names? Each name brimmed with love, the hopes and dreams of parents, and a challenge from the children who bore them to not be forgotten or have the tragedy of their death be covered up. I spent a year reading and translating. Each day, I woke up and read the names of the children whose birthday it was on that day. Choosing one or two names, I then used the etymology of the Chinese characters as a point of poetic departure. For me, the challenge was to give these names a kind of language so they could continue to speak. When I finished reading the last name, I had a year-long cycle of 366 name poems, which revealed a vast, seasonal landscape of our humanity, and of our empathy.

The title of each poem is a child's given name. Each name is preceded by the date of their birth and the transliteration of that name using pinyin so the non-Chinese speaking reader might say the name aloud should they wish. For this book, I selected 108 poems from that sequence. 108 is a number that appears again and again in the Buddhist cosmos. The number is a symbol of the wholeness of our existence and the scope of our emotions. These 108 emotions are understood as the sum of our awareness—they are what we must embrace, what we must penetrate through, and ultimately embrace again. These 108 names connote the infinity of our experience.

Acknowledgments

TWELVE YEARS PRIOR to the earthquake, in the autumn of 1995, I traveled up the Yangtze River from Shanghai to where one of its tributaries—the Min River—bubbles out of the ground in a remote valley on the eastern edge of the Tibetan plateau. Near the end of that journey, I passed through Wenchuan and Beichuan—counties near the epicenter of the earthquake. I hired a driver to take me as far as he could to the river's source. Finally, he stopped his van at a great mound of stones covered with prayer flags and said he could go no further. I ascended by foot into a little valley, following what was now a tiny stream. Near the top of the valley, there were little springs all over. I chose one, and knelt and drank. A bit of that river became part of me. The majority of children in this manuscript grew up in valleys carved by that river, and I imagine that it was an important part of their life. The year I wrote these poems, I often had a distinct sense that it was the river I was carrying within me that was writing them. The poems feel like stones dislodged from mountains and polished by the river's currents. And so, I begin my acknowledgments by extending my thanks to the Min River. And my love to the children who were killed in the earthquake and to their families.

The first draft of this set of poems was originally written on Twitter as a public conversation with Ai Weiwei and other dissidents and human rights activists who have relentlessly called for justice for these children. And during that year, many people I don't know and have never met weighed in on what I was writing, offering encouragement and insights. To them, heartfelt thanks.

It is a surprise that so little has been written about Chinese names, how they are chosen and what they might mean. When a word is removed from linguistic context, as has happened with these names, it becomes very difficult, if not impossible, to determine its exact meaning. In fact, with the lack of context, potential meanings proliferate. I probably drove many of my Chinese-speaking friends crazy as I tried to understand what a given name might mean and how I might best translate it. In particular, I would like to thank Tsering Woeser, Tang Danhong, Rong Sun, Tee Peng, Susan Huang, Lara Yang, Zhang Zhang, and Jan Willis for their generosity.

When I started writing these poems, I found myself wandering through an utterly foreign world of words, thoughts, and associations. It is easy to become lost in those shadows, and I feel fortunate to have had a set of friends to help guide me through this forest. They were also my first readers and advisors, who helped me craft some of these poems: David Axelrod, Jodi Varon, David James Duncan, Sam Hamill, and especially Jennifer Boyden. This book would simply not be what it is without you. Thank you.

And my deep gratitude to those who provided me support: to the editors at *basalt journal*, Geremie Barmé at *China Heritage*, and Yang Lian at *Survivors Poetry Journal*, who published many of the poems in this project; to Ai Weiwei Studios, in particular Darryl Leung and Jennifer Ng, who helped me sort many details and gave permission to reprint the images in this book; to the H.J. Andrews Experimental Forest and the Oak Springs Garden Foundation for the gifts of time to write and edit portions of this manuscript; to Jane and Frank Boyden, Kim Miller, Patricia Bolding, Paul Nelson, Mark Anderson, Jane Hirshfield, Charles Goodrich, Bob Wise, Katherine Krause, Andrew Quintman, Alexis Bernaut, Jocelyn Clark, Sheila Zangar, Michael Richardson and many others for their delight and encouragement along the way; to Chen Xiaowei, who translated these poems into Chinese; and to everyone at Wesleyan University Press, especially Doug Tifft and Suzanna Tamminen.

And finally, I offer special thanks to Ai Weiwei, for his commitment to the memory of these children, and for his refusal to "separate poetry from the human condition and the political process, from struggle and individual fate."

Thank you.

Index